No Hope for the Good

Written by: Brian Collins

Chapter one: The beginning

   Brandon sits all alone against a tree asleep, tired from the previous day. He wakes up to a beautiful sea of white mist in the valley down below. Brandon had forgotten how beautiful nature could be. Staring in amazement at the fog in the valley and wondering how the world could have become the way it was these days.

   The wonder ceases when he raises his hand. It is covered in crimson running down his wrist and dripping onto the leaves beside him. Everything comes rushing back to what is happening all around him and what he had done the previous day. It all started a couple of weeks ago…

…It was like any other Thursday around his little town. Wise, although it had a satellite college for the University of Virginia, was still an old sleepy coal town. There wasn't much to do around town, bowling at Pinecrest bowling alley, fishing at one of the many lakes, hunting during hunting season, or catch the latest movie at either the local theatre or the drive in when it was open. Things were looking up for the little town and companies were starting to notice the area along with the normal southern kindness and hospitality.

Things had started to get a little strange around the county and people were starting to join a new religion that had come from a combination of all of the religions combined. It was known as the Young Optimistic Understanding or YOU for short. It focused on the individual instead of others and was quite appealing. The local leader for them was very charismatic and was reaching hundreds of young and old people. His name was Charles but, everyone who knew him called him Chuck. Chuck was a stout, tall man of about 40 and you could tell he had worked hard most of his life from worn hands and arms that were muscular from using heavy tools.

Chuck held services in an old store at the local shopping center. The services would last for a couple of hours and were fairly loud. When the services were finished they wouldn't go their separate ways like most churches, but the members would have food from local stores and restaurants at a number of places to gather.

One odd thing I noticed with long standing members, was a tattoo of some sort of ancient writing it seemed. After doing some research I found it was Greek and was Chi Xi Stigma. To most it looks like crossed swords, a snake, and a scythe. Everything with the group seemed fairly normal and actually, what they were teaching was excellent for the world. Their beliefs were to not treat others as you wouldn't want to be treated and to help yourself as long as it didn't cause any issue with the family.

   This all seemed great and could help the world, which the religion was all over the world now and seemed to be gathering even the most well known people.

   This however was just fine for others but not me. I so like to treat others like I want to be treated but, I don't like indulging myself like the other part of the beliefs.

   After about a week or two a few people of the Christian community started speaking out against the new religion but, seemed to ebb after a few days and leave them alone. This didn't concern me, at first. One day after Tom, one of the members of a local church that had been speaking out against the new church was found dead on a mountain by hunters. This would have been normal, because he hunted and would often go off hunting all day and not go back home until the moon was well into the sky. The strange thing was, he had fell on an arrow while walking up a hill, or so says the coroner.

   I have went hunting with him a few times and know how and what he does in the woods. He took the hunter safety to an all time high importance. I mean he would leave his arrows in the quiver until he was fully stopped and when he used his rifle, he would not even load it until he was sitting where he was going to hunt from.

   I started asking questions about this and was quickly quieted by one of the members of the new church. The guy said he had been hunting with Tom the week before and had spotted a deer not even 30 yards away in a clearing and missed the shot because the arrow made a snapping noise when Tom had nocked the arrow. Of course this had happened many times before with us. Though still, Tom had refused to keep an arrow nocked after I had shot several deer because I always walked with mine nocked and ready. The other thing is, if he did have it nocked, he knew to walk with the arrow pointing away from him and the arrow rest was a whisker biscuit which held the arrow firmly in place.

   This was just the first of many things I started noticing.

   I went to the funeral for Tom to pay my respects to his family and their were many people there from his church. While I was there I over heard an argument in another room of the funeral home. This wasn't any old argument at all. It was Tom's wife Deidra and his 17 year old son, Jimmy. When I walked in to see if everything was ok, Deidra just nodded and started to cry.

I asked Jimmy what was going on and he replied "it's just someone who I don't think is welcome here at the funeral but, mom says dad would be the Christ like person and say forgive them!" This kind of puzzled me for a minute. Then, Deidra started to explain that it was Henry an old friend of Tom's.

See, the two if them had gotten into an argument a couple of days before Tom's accident. Henry was telling him to back off the new church, because it wasn't as bad as he thought it was. Tom, set in his ways told Henry "You don't know what I have found out!" but, Henry told him he knew everything and that he was a member of the new church.

Tom, looked at Henry in total shock and said "No, you can't be a member of that unholy group of people!" Henry then proceeded to raise his button up western shirt to show his mark. Sure enough right there on his breast was the symbol for the higher members of YOU.

Jimmy said his father just came back into the house and sat down in his tattered old grey recliner he'd had for years and started to cry. Jimmy said he had asked him why he was crying and Tom just said a friend is now a lost soul. Tom wouldn't explain what he meant by the comment he made, just that Jimmy needed to read a certain scripture in the bible.

Jimmy of course didn't pay attention to what passage his father had referred him to and at the time was really too upset to remember.

An hour later Jimmy confronted Henry and told him to come outside and talk with him. I stopped them on the way out and told them I was going to tag along just to keep the peace. Henry didn't understand but, didn't object either.

I guess the reason for not objecting is that Jimmy although only 17, was 6 ft. 2 and a stout young man. He played right defensive tackle for the local high school team and probably weighed about 250 with mostly muscle.

Once we reached the parking lot Jimmy told Henry to leave and don't come to the graveside service. Henry was stunned and asked him why.

"You're the reason he is dead you lying son of bitch!" Jimmy shouted.

"What makes you say that?" Henry asked in shock.

Jimmy starts telling him that two men from YOU, came to see Tom the day he died a couple of hours before the accident. They were dressed in jeans, leather boots, and wore a leather biker jacket with the church symbol on the left side of the chest. Henry told him that there were no men affiliated with that church that dressed that way. Jimmy insisted they were by telling him they had told Tom that they needed to talk to him about a few things with the church.

Jimmy even had used his smartphone to take a picture of them and he showed it to Henry and he didn't recognize either of the men. Henry just kept saying it had to be people who were trying to give them a bad name. Jimmy knew better, and so did I. See, I had noticed the two men around town a few times. I also started to put things together with the story Jimmy was telling.

Those same two men had been in town the day that each person who had been talking openly about how bad the new church was either disappeared or was found dead. Except for one person who was in the hospital where I work in critical condition and in a coma. They had found her in her car. She had been driving down a curvy road and came upon a patch of black ice. She died on the scene but, the EMT's revived her. The EMT that I talked to when they brought her in said the steering wheel had shoved into her chest and the air bag didn't deploy.

The odd thing about that was, I knew her. She had just bought one of those fancy Audi that was well known for it's safety and not having trouble with the air bags. She was an upstanding pillar of the community, volunteering with every group we had around to help others. The law office she owned even did court cases for free or traded in goods and labor for those who couldn't afford a lawyer and didn't want a public defender. I mean she was good as a human can get short of walking on water.

There was also one man who died in the ER right in front of me too. He was out of his mind and in severe shock. He kept screaming "666 the beast is here!" and saying the end was at hand. I wish I had paid more attention in Sunday school when I was younger. If I had of, it wouldn't have taken me long to know what he was saying. Of course most churches don't teach young children the scary stuff in the bible, just what you should do and what you shouldn't do. I never really believed in all that stuff anyway.

This guy was a construction worker and was working on top of one of the buildings at the college and had fell off and landed somehow mostly in a tree beside the building but, he had also struck the ground back first on a pile of dirt and rubble. His injuries were so severe we couldn't restrain him when he started fighting us. The only option was to sedate him and after the RN on duty gave him the sedative he still repeated the same phrase until he was out. He died a few minutes later from blood filling his lungs from the injuries.

The rest of them were either found dead and had been dead for hours. One they said had even fallen on his wrought iron fence that surrounded his house from a ladder he was on trimming his trees, which I thought was kind of odd since it was mid-November and you just don't trim trees that late in the year. To each their own though.

Henry though angry about being asked to leave his friends to wake up and not to come to the graveside services, did as he was asked and left. I didn't see Henry for a couple of days after that. When I did see him again he was in the ER because he was having chest pains and numbness in his arm.

While I was hooking up the leads for the EKG to see if he was having a heart attack, he started mentioning the conversation with Jimmy. I just talked to him like I would any other Joe who came in. He kept asking me if I believed Jimmy about him being responsible for Tom's death. I just told him it was an accident and nothing else. He insisted though that we talk about it. So I started talking about it and told him I had seen those two guys around town a few times. I also told him about the day I saw him talking to them. That was a mistake, because he had been having a heart attack and had one right there in front of me. It was a good thing though because we brought him back and stabilized him for transport to a bigger hospital with an heart specialist.

He had to have surgery to bypass a couple of blocked arteries but, he made it through it all. When I went to see him at the hospital, he said he was sorry. I told him no need to apologize, that I had caused the stress on him by giving in and talking about the stuff. Henry told me not that, but about everything.

He explained he had a near death experience and was explained that the group he was with was not the answer but, the problem. Of course I just blew it off as him feeling guilty for not being honest about the men. He explained that the new church had recruited him as a sort of planner for different things. He wouldn't tell me exactly what he had been planning for them, he just said it wasn't all good.

Henry started telling me that they knew Tom had found out some of the stuff he had been planning. He also insisted they didn't have anything to do with Tom's death that those two men are just instructors and messengers for the church. They wear their clothing like that because they were once part of a 1%er motorcycle club and wanted to show they were converted to the good. This seemed to be legitimate and made sense. After all what better way to reach the wolves but, to send in wolves.

His surgery went really well and he was recovering very well. Then one day I got a message that he had died of a complication from the surgery. This didn't happen often, but it did happen. At the wake I saw his brother who was there the day he died and he said he was sitting up talking one second and the next he just grabbed his chest, his eyes rolled back into his head and he slumped over. The way he described it sounded like a blood clot had made it past all the precautions that were taken.

As his brother walked away though he said "and even after two of his really nice church buddies left!"

One after another I started noticing a pattern and possibly a connection between all of the deaths.

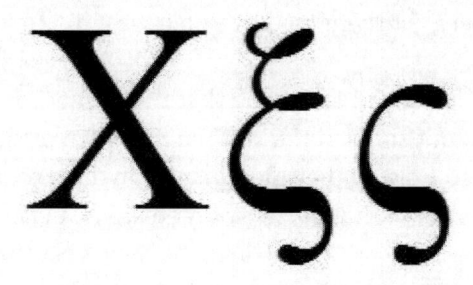

Χέςς

Chapter two: Pieces of the Puzzle

I started doing a little research on my own after talking to Henry's brother.

The first thing I did was make sure that I did this without drawing attention to myself and making sure of this. Working at one of only three hospitals within a 15 mile radius helps to get some of the information I was looking for. Although the medical records are not public information, if you work at a medical facility as a medical associate, you can get access to it. I looked up all the people who had passed away within the last few weeks.

I started noticing that a lot of them were accidents alone. I mean, for this little area 15 or 20 a month of these type of accidents happen but not 20 in just 2 and a half weeks.

One guy had stepped outside on a cold day, it had been raining the evening before and ice had formed a lot of places. The cause of death was an icicle piercing his left eye and into his brain. One had been mowing and fell off his tractor and the tiller ran over him after the back wheel had crushed his skull. Another had been cleaning his rifle and it went off sending the cleaning rod through the bottom of his mouth and out through the top of his skull.

Things just were not really what they seemed. I mean really, this guy was a Marine. It is pounded into your brain how to and how not to clean your rifle.

   That was just a start too. There were decapitations, accidental poisonings, even a smoking in bed death. Did the local police not see a pattern here or did they just not want to. After all one of the deaths was a deputy for the county police for God's sake.

   I also discovered that all of the deaths the people were alone at the time. Well, I knew curiosity killed the cat but, I'm not a cat. I started digging as far as I could go into the records and found everyone that had died of an accident during that time. There were a lot too.

   I started talking to relatives of those people. I was telling them it was "a follow up on services provided" so I wouldn't really draw attention to myself. Everyone I talked to had a few things in common to say. All of those who had died were visited by the two men in leather jackets.

   I knew then something was up for sure and knew I had better start carrying my 45 I had purchased after 10 years in the Marines. I also carried my loyal and trusty Kabar beside the seat in my Jeep. I had never since I was in thought I needed to carry those, until now. I mean if these two guys were the "messengers" for YOU, I don't think I want what they are saying.

After finding out all I could about the deaths I started looking into who these guys were. When I started looking into who they were I ran into a road block with every turn. The first was when I retrieved the picture from Jimmy and decided to do a picture search. I found several images of them but, no names. These two had been all over the east coast and seen by many.
What I don't understand is, how in the hell do these guys go around and don't have a public profile on one of the social media sites. Yet they have pictures taken by hundreds of people on their pages. Then I noticed one of the pictures was from a local person and they belonged to YOU. They had names on the picture. Finally I had a break, the first names only, but it was a start. They were not wearing the jackets though. They both were stocky but, one had blonde hair and the other had black hair. The blonde was had the name of John tagged and Pete was the other.

I thought to myself that it was strange for them to have those names. After all that was 2 of the disciples from the bible, but that was what names I found information about them. Pete, was Peter Wilson and had a list 3 pages long of crimes he had committed and prison time he had spent. This was a really colorful character to say the least. Most of his offenses were assault and battery and from what a State Police friend told me he had been an enforcer for the Satan's Seed's MC. John wasn't much better, he had the same kind of crimes but, not as many listed. John's name was John Mueller and he also was an enforcer for the same MC. These two, if people were being murdered, would explain why these two were visiting then before hand.

   I finally got hold of the coroners reports for all the deceased from the last couple of weeks. This was interesting reading. I noticed not all of the pieces of the puzzle added up with them. I mean, the one for Tom, it stated that the arrow went through his left eye socket and exited the back of his head and had been from Tom holding it in his left hand. He was left handed yes, although a left hand person would hold their bow in their left hand and have an arrow in the right if they were holding the arrow. If they had the arrow nocked, the nock would have went into his eye and not the broad head of the arrow.

   The gentleman who had fell off the building had deep tissue bruising that was consistent with a boxer or MMA fighter. It kind of seemed like he had been beaten before he fell. Maybe he didn't fall, maybe he was thrown off the building. Then along with that he had what appeared to be rope burns on his wrists and ankles.

The more I read, the more I started thinking Jimmy was right about Tom and Henry.

Even the man who had the icicle through his eye had suspicious markings on him. He lived alone but, there was a meal for two people there in his dining room. Was he suppose to meet someone or was there someone who is a witness to the crime we don't know about. Anyway, he had the same rope burns on him.

After scanning through all the files, all of them but the woman had rope burns on their wrists and ankles. The woman though had a daughter who was in her 20's and she had asked if anyone had seen the silk scarf her mother always wore. Maybe that was used instead, after all silk would be much less likely to leave a mark on the skin.

There were two who were decapitated, one woman and a husband and wife in the same vehicle. Both also had the rope burns on their wrists and ankles. The car had been speeding and he lost control and went under a parked tractor and trailer. They hit the trailer so hard it knocked it of the back of the truck and ripped the bottom of the trailer halfway off. It was late at night on a road most don't travel and no where near anyone they knew or their home. What was even odder about the accident is that when the police investigated the scene, there was the end of a bungee cord in the car but, the owner of the truck said he didn't have any on his truck. The victim's family said they had never seen them use one either. There was also a symbol burnt into the gentleman's arm. The police just marked it up to the airbag but, the coroner said it looked more like a tribal tattoo burnt into his skin.

   When I read this I decided to go back through all of the files once again and see if the others had some sort of odd marks on them other than the rope burns.

   Sure enough, each one had some sort of brand like mark on them.

   The coroner had taken pictures of each of the marks, so it was kind of easy to look them up once they were visualized from the pictures. Some of them looked fairly fresh and very red so it was kind of hard to tell what they were. The rest were plain as day what they were. It was really easy to figure out the ones that weren't clear after I figured out they were. Each one was a symbol from Greek writing, either a zodiac sign or a letter from the Greek alphabet. Some were tiny and unless you knew what to look for you would just assume it was a scar or a little burn. Others were large enough to see detail.

   Tom had one too, it was on his under arm, just a little below his armpit. It was like the symbol for a male but had a crescent facing up on the top. When I looked that symbol up, it was a symbol for Hades. Why on earth would a preacher have or even get the symbol for Hades on them. I had known him for years and never have seen it on him.

The guy who was killed by the icicle had ironically, what looked like a spear shape on the side of his index finger toward the inside of the hand. After looking up this symbol I found out it was the symbol for Sagittarius and was an arrow.

The decapitated couple both had the same one. Hers was on the inside of her thigh, small and very inflamed. It looked kind of like the symbol for Pi with an extra line at the bottom. This one I knew right away and didn't have to look it up at all, it was Gemini.

The markings seemed to mean something. What I hadn't figured out yet.

Things were starting to become clearer and clearer the more I read. There were a few things that had me stumped though, why the marks on the bodies and what did they mean? At this point I started back talking to people who knew them and EMS workers who had responded to the calls.

With all this information swirling around in my head, I couldn't help but ask questions of the church members. I knew it would draw attention to what I was doing but, I needed answers.   Most of the members were very talkative but, very secretive about the deaths. One in particular was a gentleman whom I had known most of my life. We called him pops, because we had all looked up to him growing up and he was like a father to most of us.

   Pops when I asked him about the markings the first time he just changed the subject to something about hunting. Of course I didn't give up, not yet anyway. I answered all he was asking me about hunting from how many squirrel I had killed during squirrel season, to the deer I got a couple of years back. Then I asked him about one of the markings, the Sagittarius.

   He said "Oh, I know what that is. That is the sign of the zodiac, hmm. They musta got it as their birth sign."

   I told him I had thought the same thing, but the one that had it, weren't that birth sign. I told him who it was and he agreed that was odd. After talking to him for what seemed to be several hours, I had to go to work. I shook his hand and told him it had been great talking to him. As I walked off he said "It's been great talking to you too and Brandon, you watch yourself out there. There are some crazy people in this world. Now you don't want to end up on the wrong end of one of those beds do you?" This seemed quite odd for him to tell me, especially since we had just been talking about the accidents.

While I was at work I started talking to a coworker about what I had found and what I thought. She was a member of one of the local churches and also was a history buff. I showed her a few things that I had found when I got the chance and she was very interested in it all. As the night went on and our shift was almost over she called me over to the medicine room and shut the door.

She started trying to tell me some things she had found from the information I had shared.

"The first thing I did was start looking up the symbols. The zodiac and the other symbols mean different things. The one Tom had meant he was the devil and lied. The Gemini meant they were two faced and couldn't be trusted. The Sagittarius was for someone who meant to destroy something. The one that concerns me the most is the one that the YOU church higher members wear. That symbol is also a Greek symbol but, it is also writing and is numbers. It is the numbers six hundred sixty and 6." She spat out.

I looked at her kind of puzzled. She shook her head in disbelief.

"Bran, it is 666, you know 'the number of the beast, for it is man's number' from revelations? Don't you remember that from church?" she said in disbelief.

After she said that things started making more sense and the pieces of the puzzle started to fall into place.

Chapter Three: A beg for help

This wasn't any ordinary cult, this was a serious force to deal with. If they were using the symbol for the beast as their symbol, then they were evil and something needed to be done. I didn't know where to go and what to do.

If I go to the town police they will laugh at me and tell me to go home and don't worry about it. If I go to the sheriff's office I am liable to be shipped of to Marion at the state mental hospital. If I go to the state police office they will just put it in the pile of complaints and issues they have and it may be months, even years before anything is done.

Then again, who with those agencies could be trusted and who couldn't.

I was on my own once again and only had one person I could confide in and she is put in danger by knowing all of this.

I went home at the end of my shift and locked all the locks on my door and got a 45 automatic I had in a lock box and put it under my pillow. The night went by fairly fast and was uneventful. I heard a noise outside around eleven or so but, it was just an opossum in my trash can having his nightly snack.

The next morning I decided I was going to talk to a few more people and see if I could figure out a few more things. As I walked out of the house I noticed a foul odor coming from under the front porch. This wasn't anything unusual, because I lived out away from most people and there were several animals that would come around to check out what I had thrown away. Some of them would stay under my porch and of course another animal would find them and kill them. This would leave a rotting corpse under my porch for me to find.

I went to the garage and got a shovel, flashlight, and some lime dust I had just for this reason. See, lime dust covers the smell somewhat and also assists in the rapid decay of the flesh.

When I crawled under the porch I found what had died was what looked like a large rat. Scooping it up with the shovel, I drug it out into the sunlight and it stunk worse than when I first found it. As it came into the light I noticed it was actually an opossum which looked like it had been skinned alive and left for dead. Right as I was about to cover it with the lime dust, I noticed what looked like a brand on its side.

Oh my god, it was a brand and looked like the same symbol that Tom had on him. I took out my phone and snapped a picture of it and quickly covered it with lime. At least the smell was gone for the most part and the rotting animal would be gone soon too.

Right as I was about to leave to check into a few more things my phone rang. It was the hospital and they wanted me to come in and work another shift even though it was my day off. It seemed that my coworker had not shown up for work today and no one could get hold of her. This was really odd because we had just spoke the night before and she was looking forward to the shift today. She lived alone too and her boyfriend worked as a janitor at the hospital and he worked today too.

   I walked in to work reluctantly and as I did Gene her boyfriend asked me if she had said anything about not being in tonight or if she was going somewhere. Of course I told him she was looking forward to the shift with him.

   I tried several times to reach her on her cell phone but, she didn't answer any calls and every text was delivered, but not read. It was like she didn't want to be bothered, so I just left it alone.

   Every time Gene came through the ER he would ask if I had heard from her and of course I hadn't. This started to worry me some. She had never gone this long without messaging me or Gene. She would always send me silly pictures or jokes through messenger or text at least 4 or 5 times a day. After a few hours past Gene had finished almost all of his work he had to do and came by to talk. He asked me what we had talked about the night before.

Of course I told him about our theories and all we had discussed. He showed me the message she had sent earlier in the day. My eyes were kind of blurry though from the lack of sleep and I had to move the phone closer to see the letters.

"Man you're getting old Brandon. You have to get you some reading glasses before you go blind, old man." Gene joked as he nudged me with his elbow.

After reading the text I started to really worry. It was telling him that she had been at the library reading about the symbols and doing some research to give me. Then on her way home two guys were following her. See she lived just down the hill from the library in some 70's style apartments owned by the local hardware store owner. They were not very big, but they were big enough for a single woman to live in. They were painted a tan color and had the slant roofs like a lean to would have. They didn't have many windows in them or much of any discerning characteristics other than they were plain and had the slant roofs.

She mentioned these guys kind of looked like bikers and she just got in her car and drove off so she could lose them. Nothing else was sent after that. Gene had sent several texts after that though like anyone who cared for a person and was concerned for them.

I told him a little more about what her and I had discussed and he mentioned the one librarian was a member of that new church. He knew this because his sister was a librarian also and had talked about her asking about trying the new church. At that point I really started to almost panic. My heart started beating faster, my breathing became shallow, and at that point Gene got a chair and sat me down.

"You know something you're not telling me, don't you." Gene stammered.

"Yes." Came out slow and quietly.
I began to tell him everything we had found out and what she was probably looking for. His eyes got teary and he sat down in a chair across from me. He sat with his head in his hands and started to cry.

Reassuring him that she would be fine because she had gotten away from them like she did, I laid my hand on his shoulder. Of course it wasn't just to calm him down it was to reassure myself.

Time seemed to drag on slowly as the end of the shift came closer and closer. When the shift finally ended Gene and I knew we'd see each other later and hoped it would be on better terms than what had happened during the shift.

We walked out of the medicinal smelling building and made our way to our cars. As I was going to start the car my phone started playing AC-DC's "back in black" and that kind of startled me, because of all the things Gene and I had talked about.

A voice softly and panicky whispered "come get me" from the other end as I answered it. I knew the voice it was Julia, my coworker. She had an ominous desperation in her voice. She began to tell me she was in the woods in a little cubbyhole where equipment was behind Midway High School.

She had told me how exactly to find her down to what was in front of the cubbyhole and what color the piece of metal was. After all there were multiple pieces of old dilapidated equipment in behind the school. After all it was the junk yard for the county and an old construction company that had been owned by the McGinnis family.

See the McGinnis' were a prominent family in the area that owned and still owns several businesses and buildings. They not only owned part of the land where the school now sits but, they also were the kind of family that if someone needed something they would try to provide it as long as they deserved it.

I arrived at the school and parked after making sure no one was around and walked into the junk yard. I walked past the old loader she had described and then the bulldozer with only one arm. The hardest thing to find was the old bus hood but, I found it and to the left was the oil drums stacked just like she had described. And of course there was the sheer metal she told me would be there that had the smiley face painted on it.

"Julia, it's me Brandon. I am here to take you wherever you need to go." Then a faint sound of crying came from behind the piece of what looked like an old heating duct and a shaking voice. No one followed you did they and you are alone right?"

I moved the metal out of the way and there she was cowering under another piece of metal. She was dirty and her clothes were torn but, she seemed to be alright other than the fact she was scared so bad she was trembling.

I helped her get out of the dirt floor cubbyhole she was in and started to brush off the dead grass, leaves, and dirt from her tattered clothes. As I brushed across her right thigh she cringed and pulled away. I knew she was injured and needed a strong drink to calm her down.

We started walking toward the car and I mentioned going to the hospital to get her checked out and she stopped in her tracks. "No, we have to go somewhere no one knows about and I have to hide from them!" she nervously spouted. I reassured her it would be ok that we could go in a side entrance and get supplies to fix her up but, she insisted we not go to the hospital. "The only other place to go would be to my house." I explained. She only wanted me to go in and get the necessary supplies and come back out though.

I really didn't like that idea but, she wouldn't have it any other way. So once we had settled on what we were going to do, we made our way to the car. She made me check around for anyone looking or even walking by before she would walk out into the open.

Something must have really spooked her for her to be acting like she was. She never scared easy, even in scary movies she would laugh at others jumping from being scared.

When I opened the door for her to get in she crawled into the back floorboard and waited for me to shut the door. When I shut the door Julia grabs a blanket from the back seat and lays down in the floorboard. I walked back around the car watching as though I was doing a drug deal or completing a mission with the CIA. As I settle into the plush velour feeling seat a car comes around the building and they wave at me. In the back floorboard I can hear Julia starting to hyperventilate. I reassured her by my voice as I acknowledge the assistant football coach by saying his name and waving to him.

   Nothing at all would be thought of by him, because I always would come up there to just be alone and clear my mind in the woods behind the school. He just drove on by and went about his day and I am guessing he was going to check on the locker room and the equipment for practice that evening.

   I started the car up, shut the door, and drove off. Julia calmed down more and more the further we got away from the school. Although she had calmed down, once I pulled into my drive she almost lost it. I had to calm her down and let her know that it was either we came here or we went to the hospital to get supplies to patch her up and see what was wrong with her. She panicked begging me not to leave her In the car and also refusing to go in. I reassured her I would be just a couple of minutes and that my kit was just inside the door and another thing I needed to get was just in the next room from there.

   She calmed down once again and asked me to please hurry.

I rushed in the door, grabbed my med kit, and ran to the bedroom to get my 45 and the holster for it. As I ran by the window I noticed one of the biker guys walking around the other side of the house. It seemed as if he were looking for something, or someone. I hurried out the door, which was just the opposite way he was going, making sure not to make a loud noise with the door. I hurried to the car, I didn't want to scare Julia, so I didn't mention the biker guys. I started the car backed out of the drive, and when I do the biker guys come from around the house. I put the car in drive and floor it, spinning the tires when I did.

The first thing she asked when I did that was "Why did you do that which at that moment I had to tell her. "I saw the biker guys at my house and they were coming toward the car. Everything is ok now." This made her start to panic and hyperventilate. The further we got away from there the calmer she got.

I asked her where we could go if she didn't want to go home or my house. Her answer was "I don't know, you choose." Pf course I couldn't think of any place to go that wouldn't be associated with Julia or I either one. Then it dawned on me My cousins had a cabin on High Knob that was on top of a hill away from everything and very secluded. It was perfect! No one knew about it but family and no one would be there because hunting season was over, not to mention to get there you needed a 4 wheel drive that was fairly high off the ground. Luckily I knew of such 4 wheel drive that I had in storage at the bottom of the mountain in an old garage.

  I stopped at the garage and she made sure no one was around before she got out of the car. She slowly made her way out of the car and limped to the garage. I had pulled over to the side of the garage so I could back the truck out. It wasn't anything to look at, as a matter of fact it was just an old Dodge Power Ram I had painted flat black and only had a blackout roll bar. The truck as a matter of fact kind of smelled like moth balls a bit. I hadn't driven it for 2 months, because I only used it to get to the cabin and hunt.

  I turned the key and it came to life, roaring like a lion. The sound kind of startled Julia and she jumped. The truck ran just as good as the day I put the engine in it, see I always had a secret craving, desire or whatever you want to call it. The first time I ever watched "Simon & Simon" as a kid, I knew what kind of vehicle I wanted and what I would have eventually. I found this beauty in a junk yard almost ready to be scrapped and saved her, kind of like Julia.

I found all the parts to match the "macho" upgrades for the truck on the show and all. It took me a few years to find everything. I even bought the original red paint that was on that one. Even though I hadn't painted the truck I still loved it and protected it. This of course was my baby and no one was going to hurt her.

I backed out of the garage and pulled over to the side, enough to get my car in there. Julia crawled into the truck and waited for me to come back. I locked the double doors on the garage and hopped back into the truck where Julia was asleep already. Halfway up the mountain Julia jumps up hitting her head on the roof of the truck.

"Careful with Mimi, she is tough but you'll dent the roof with that hard head of yours!" I half jokingly said.

Of course Julia with whom I had worked with for going on 5 years knew why my truck was called Mimi and the whole story behind why I have it. After all that is almost all I talked about for 4 or 5 months when I got her.

Julia just grinned and smiled. "Not much further to the cabin she knew how long it was to get there because she and I had ran away a couple of years back to hide from an old boyfriend of hers who was very abusive. I always had a CB radio base station there and solar panels with windmill backup power. Just so I didn't have to go too native while being there.

As I pulled up to the cabin I started remembering the first times coming up there for her and I. No sooner than I put Mimi in park, and cut her off, Julia was opening the door and sliding out of the door. There was a little snow on the ground from a light snowfall we had a couple of weeks ago. It looked pristine and majestic at least until we walked across it.

I was glad the snow was there, it let me know that no one had been there in a while. I opened the door and that familiar odd old wood and gun oil smell came from inside. To most that smell would not be too pleasant to the nose, but I loved it.

Julia walks right in and plops down on the couch, rustling the blanket my mom had made me years ago. I closed the door and nudged her slightly "no laying down just yet. I have to check you out to see what all is wrong. Come on, you know how trauma assessment goes!"

She reluctantly moved the covers back and sat up.

"You won't like one thing you see. Trust me, you won't!" she muttered.

"It doesn't matter if I like it or not, I still have to make sure you're ok. What could be so bad that I wouldn't like it?" I said kidding around. Julia wasn't wrong though. She slowly unbuttoned her jeans and slid her pants down to show her thigh.

I dropped everything and it would be safe to say that I had a look of total horror and disbelief on my face. Starting right there in my face was something I had never thought I would see on someone living or that would he living this long. There on her thigh was a brand, not any other brand was like this, it looked like a crow sitting on an apple.

"Oh my god, what happened and what the hell is that?" I blurted out before thinking.

Julia began to tell me about what she had found out and what all had happened to her. She had chosen the wrong people to trust. She didn't say exactly who it was she had trusted but, went on to tell me that the symbol was for some obscure Greek goddess named Atë. She was the goddess of delusion and rash actions.

I asked her how in the hell she got away from those two goons and she said it was dumb luck. They had to go take care of something else quickly and she was tied up to a chair but, when they tried her she used a trick she learned as a child growing up. Julia had wanted to be a magician when she grew up so she read every book she could find. One of these books was a book on escape. I kept thinking that it was a good thing she did. It was an excellently written book too, I had read it and magic tricks was how we started talking more.

See one night we had a little boy who had been playing and fell in his yard. The bad thing was his parents were remodeling and the front porch wasn't quite finished and had pieces of rebar sticking up where they were going to pour concrete the next day. The rebar had went through his shoulder and had to be removed but, he was terrified of needles and we had to start an IV. In order to keep him calm and occupied I started doing slight of hand tricks and it worked.

   It also caught the interest of one nurse. Julia wouldn't stop talking about illusions and escape tricks and books she had read, so I had to read them. See in that book it tells you the secret to escaping from ropes is to tense up and make your body bigger by doing so. That way when the ropes are tied they are loose and it makes it easier to slip out of them.

Chapter Four: The worst case scenario

After assuring Julia that no one would find us and letting her know that we had enough to eat and then some, she relaxed and fell asleep.

I started making something to eat for her and I. I hadn't eaten in about 5 or 6 hours and I know she hadn't had anything to eat even longer. This actually reminded me of when we had stayed there a few years before. The smell of the food evidently pleases her senses by arriving at her nose and tickling her taste buds because, she sat up and came to the kitchen.

"Mmm, that smells wonderful. Remind me again why you didn't got to culinary school instead of nursing school." Julia said with a sarcastic voice.

"You know why I didn't, I had to stay around here to help with dad when he fell and broke his neck." I responded. My father had been cleaning the gutters on the house and fell of the ladder onto his neck. I thought he was fine until he said he was tired and was going to lay down. He went to get back up and couldn't move. After the doctor at the hospital said he would never walk again and we had to watch about what we fed him as to not suffocate him. He lived just long enough for me to graduate nursing school and start a job at a nursing

We sat down at the small table and she started eating, and I could tell she was hungry. If she hadn't of been using a fork you would've thought she was raised by a pack of wild animals. Once we finished our food (which she had 3 helpings of), we went over to the couch and began talking about what had happened.

After what seemed to be hours we got sidetracked by an awesome memory of the last time we were at the cabin. She even remembered what we ate that day and what I wore, down to the smell of my cologne. I remembered the food and how she cuddled up to me after the meal. "I have a little secret though, you may get mad about it. Then again, you may be happy came from her sort of reluctantly. "You know how we laid back and you held me? Well I decided right then and there to find a man just like you. One that cared about me and would protect me and not hurt me." Which made me feel good about myself.

She leaned over to kiss me and I turned my head so she would kiss my cheek. She jerked back "Don't you want to kiss me." Which she sounded a little irritated with me at that moment. I couldn't do that because she was dating Gene and that just wouldn't be right.

    "Is it because of Gene? If so don't worry, we aren't together after yesterday. Oh, I forgot to tell you the most important part of my whole ordeal yesterday. That son of a bitch is with that church!" You could have heard a pin hit a tile floor for just a second or two but, seemed like an eternity.

    She was telling me about the one biker being Gene's brother and that she had been telling Gene about what we had found out so far. Also about me not knowing what she had found out and he had went to the kitchen to get some coffee and called his brother to come there. She hadn't of thought anything about it until Gene helped them tie her up and also was the one to brand her.

    I told her about how he had acted at work and seemed really concerned about her. All of this was just a front and a cover up for getting me to tell what I had uncovered. Why would he do that though? He had turned on someone who he had cared about. What kind of people were these YOU church members.

Julia of course found out Gene was the right hand man for Chuck. Gene had given the information to recruit his brother for a sort of cleaner. Gene's brother belonged to one if the 1%er motorcycle clubs that was well known for making problems disappear for good. Of course he would have the knowledge to get rid of problem people for the church and probably had done it for several years with the MC.

Things were starting to really make sense now and everything was falling into place. I at that moment realized that we needed to move to another place. I had a little hunting hut up the hill from the cabin that had a place to sleep, a heater, and a place to go to the bathroom. It didn't have much but, would provide an excellent shot if someone came up to the cabin.

I gathered up some extra blankets, food, and a few other supplies and we headed up to the hut. It was a hard walk with all of that stuff but, we made it. We set everything up and sat hugging until the heater warmed the crisp air in the hut. Once it earned up she asked me why we had to move to the hut.

   I explained to her I had been talking to Gene the night she didn't come to work and had told him about the cabin. "I told him about the time we spent up here away from your ex and he asked where it was. I didn't tell him where it was because he was called away for a clean up and didn't get to come back down until the shift was over."

   She started to panic a little bit and at that moment I noticed an old Ford Bronco coming up the road and I didn't recognize it at all. I grabbed my rifle and told Julia to be ready to hand me another one just in case.

   The vehicle was pretty pristine considering it's age. When I looked through the scope I saw 3 men in there, Gene, and the two bikers. When they pulled up to the cabin they all got out and started to look around the place. One of them even went in and came right back out. They looked around the place. Luckily I knew a few things about hiding tracks and had tied a couple of pine branches to my belt on either side to brush our tracks away. It looked like they weren't going to leave anytime soon.

Just when I thought they were going to come out way, the one biker got a call and he motioned for Gene and the other guy to come on. They hopped into the Bronco and drove off. I told her to wait there and I needed to check something real quick. I didn't tell her I had left a note saying that I was my uncle and I had gone out looking for deer and turkeys.

I walked in the cabin and sure enough the note was crumpled up on the floor and I noticed a smell I recognized. The guy had thrown a dirty oil soaked rag on the gas stove. I turned and ran out as I got to the yard the house exploded into flames. I guess they were making sure no one was staying there. They didn't know about the little hut I had. Which we couldn't stay in long because the wood I had for it was behind the cabin and was on fire along with the cabin.

Stupid me didn't think about the cabin burning down and put it near the shed. Of course who would think about that. I hurried back to the hut and as I walked in the Bronco came back up the road. This time it only had Gene and one of the bikers. They stopped a little bit back from the cabin and sat and watched it burn.

   I guess they were waiting on the person who was hunting to come back. The biker got out of the driver's seat and started walking g towards the cabin. At that exact moment I realized my error.

   I had forgotten to cover my tracks the second time. He looked up towards us and started walking our way. Gene started to get out and I heard the biker tell him to stay the hell with the bronco. Gene sat back down but, left the door open.

   The biker started walking towards us again following the tracks. The closer he got the more Julia panicked. I put my hand on her shoulder and whispered. It will be okay. I aimed at the guy right at his chest like my uncle had taught me. I knew if I aimed at his head I could miss a lot easier than at his chest. I put my finger on the trigger and started the squeeze (my uncle had taught me how to shoot and trained me the way he was trained as a U.S.M.C. Scout sniper.) I took a breath and at the top of it I finished the squeeze and the shot rang out through the mountains. As I saw the biker drop I turned the rifle to Gene.

Gene wasn't stupid he got down and crawled over to the driver's seat and started the Bronco. Without raising up he put it in reverse and started backing down the road almost taking out a few trees on his way. He got down to where there were trees blocking my view and I could see him raise up and start to look where he was going.

I looked over at Julia and she was just sitting there in shock. I put my hands on both sides of her shoulders and gently shook her. "What was that for? Why did you shake me?"

"I thought you were in shock" the words came out abruptly.

"I was just amazed by the way you just handled that, I never knew you had it in you." Julia responded.

I started to slyly grin "Now one problem. Where can we go now, I mean, we just let them know we were here by doing that."

Chapter Five: the new hideout

   She began to explain that there was another place on the mountain we might be able to go to but, it would be kind of hard to get to. This kind of puzzled me, because I knew she didn't hunt and that no one in her family did as far as I knew. I just simply trusted her to know where to go and follow where she was going to lead me. Even though I would be basically flying blind and didn't know where she was thinking of.

   We gathered up all the supplies and the weapons and took them to the truck. On the way I stopped to make sure the biker was actually dead, sure enough the shot had went right through his heart and he wasn't breathing. I told her we would have to be careful and make sure Gene wasn't at the bottom waiting on us. She agreed and as we drove at a snail's pace down the hill, she watched the road ahead for the Bronco. We made it to the bottom and no sign of Gene anywhere.

She told me to turn right into the main road and just keep going until she said to turn. We drove it seemed for several miles but, with the road being rough it could've been just a couple. We came upon a road that looked like it hadn't been traveled in quite some time. It had ruts in it where rain had washed down the road and you could tell it had gravel on it at one time. Julia yells "here, turn here."

I quickly turned up the raggedy road and we slowly made our way up it. About a half a mile up the road it had been washed out by water running across it. I stopped and got out to assess the crevasse. It wasn't too bad from what I saw, just a quick run at it should allow us to make it across. I hopped back into the truck and explained to Julia what I was going to do.

"Are you sure we can make it, I mean what if we get stuck? We are out in the middle of no where." Julia questionably responded.

"Trust me, been there, done that. I have jumped bigger gaps than this before." I said with confidence. When in the back of my mind the whole time I was thinking " oh god, I hope we make it.!"

I backed down the road far enough to get a good run and go at it, put both hands on the wheel, and put the truck in 4-wheel high. Looking around at Julia "Hold my beer, let's do this!" (this was a little joke between us, being from a small town, "hold my beer" is known as the famous last words of a redneck.)

I gave the truck just enough gas to pull out quickly but, not spin the wheels and sped up quickly. We got to the edge of the huge rut and I had to fight closing my eyes. We went airborne for a few seconds and then I felt the front wheels grab the rocky road on the other side. With a thud the back wheels hit the edge of the rut and we were across.

Julia let out a deep sigh and said it wasn't much further. Of course she was right, because about a mile past the rut sat a huge, what looked like a mansion of a cabin.

"What is this place, and how did you know about it?" I asked in sort of amazement.

Julia explained that it was an old retreat for one of the wealthier people in town and her and her ex use to go there to have time to themselves. I didn't care as long as we could have heat and stay dry.

We carefully went in the door because the porch looked as though it had not been used in years or taken care of. There were boards broken and some even missing. Once we opened the door though , it looked amazing, dusty but amazing. It looked as if someone had been using it off and on for a while. This kind of concerned me. I mean I didn't want anyone to walk in and have to shoot another person.

Then Julia spoke up "I can see by your face you are concerned. Don't be! You know how I disappear from time to time? Well, here is where I go, and don't worry, Gene doesn't know about this place!"

My nerves started to calm down and I relaxed a little. "Go ahead, look around the place. It's really awesome. Just stay out of the bedroom upstairs to the right." Julia happily spouted.

"Why is that where you keep your stash or is it you have a dead body in there?" I said laughing.

"Nope, but the raccoons that live in there will make you wish you had of listened!" Julia said smirking.

I did look around for a few minutes. The kitchen was fully stocked, the bathroom had running water and linen, the beds had sheets on them and blankets. I asked her why it was I like this and she explained that she set it up as a sort of retreat of her own and had talked the owners into letting her use it and turn the utilities on, if she paid them. She had been doing that for quite some time now.

"You have, or had your cabin to retreat to and I have mine. Which you can use now too." Julia said with a smile.

I knew that smile and I was glad to see it. She hadn't smiled like that since right before we had discussed the symbols. It was getting late and she told me that I could have the bedroom straight ahead at the top of the stairs and she would take the one to the left.

I made my way to the middle bedroom and laid down on the bed after changing into a pair of shorts to sleep in. I had been laying there thinking of what we would do the next day and I heard a gentle knock on the door. I got up and opened it to see Julia in a pair of shorts and a tank top.

"Is it ok if I sleep in here tonight, I don't feel safe in that bedroom alone or on the couch?" Julia shyly asked.

"Of course, I'll sleep on the floor and you can have the bed." I gentlemanly answered.

"No need there is enough room in the bed for the both of us." Julia stated "Enough to have space between us, or not to have space between us."

The both of us settled in the bed and I put my 45 under my pillow before I laid back down. As I did she inched over to me and snuggled close. I didn't mind this because I did find her attractive but, I did not want to lose a good friend. I always kept it as friends, because I had been friends with a woman before and we had started dating and drifted apart, then a nasty breakup left her almost an enemy. I didn't want this with Julia.

I slept on edge all night and every thud or rustling I heard I woke up and looked around to make sure we were alone. It didn't help that the raccoons in the next room were active, I mean very active. I may have gotten 2 or 3 hours sleep again. I knew the next day would be horrible but, at least we were safe, for now.

The next morning we got up, fixed breakfast and made sure everything was locked down right. After 2 or 3 cups of coffee, she mentioned a place to pull the truck to behind the cabin. I cranked the truck up and pulled around the back and right there was a little carport. It had plywood bolted on the sides and cedar siding on that. When I pulled into the carport I noticed over to the side a little shed.

Of course me being curious, I checked it out. It had several ordinary things in it along with a few odd and not very normal for a shed at a cabin. I noticed a wooden box that looked like it wasn't too old but you could tell it was fairly well used. I pulled the small cover that draped over it and to my surprise I saw the letters TNT on the side. I opened it expecting just some old junk to be stored in it. That was totally wrong. It had several sticks of dynamite, a couple of blocks of c4, a claymore mine, trip wire and a few detonators.

I picked up the box and took it inside to show Julia. She didn't seem surprised by it.

"That was something Richard put in there when we came up here." Julia spouted.

Richard was the ex she had hidden from before and he was kind of an outlaw and did a lot of illegal things I knew about and most I didn't want to know about. All I knew was I was glad this was there. I asked her if anyone would be coming up here to the cabin and she assured me there wouldn't be. So I let her know what I was about to do with all of this. I was going to set traps and mines for anyone who decided to come up there. She grabbed her coat and told me she was coming with me.

After about an hour or two we set about five or six booby traps around the front side of the cabin far enough away as to not hit the cabin with anything but close enough to see it. A couple of them were just a chunk of c4 with a detonator and a small board on top of it covered in leaves. Then a couple were a chunk of c4 on the side of a tree and a detonator with a tripwire going to a rock for the trigger. And of course the claymore we put at the bottom of the steps aimed out towards the drive.

   This was something that we needed to do but, did not want to have to do. Two or three days went by and nothing out of the ordinary happened. Then we heard one of the traps go off. It made a war busting boom and then a few seconds later dirt and other debris started falling on the cabin. I looked out of the window slowly and every so slightly moving the curtain. I kept watching for any sign of someone coming up the road or walking through the woods.

   Nothing was moving, until I saw what looked like something black moving up the hill a little to the right of where the blast was. At first I thought it might be a bear, then I noticed something shiny. It was the other biker, and right there with him was Gene, both were covered in dirt and blood splatter. It looked as if they had someone else with them and it was them that tripped the explosives. How did they know to come here though, how do they know about this place? Julia saw the guys and quietly hurried over and grabbed the rifles and motioned for me to follow her. I crawled over her way and she moved the rug back a little bit and there in the floor was a door and the couch was right over it. We moved the couch up a small amount, just enough to get through the trap door. Once inside what I expected to be a cellar, in fact was another room. It was complete even a toilet and lighting. The ceiling was solid without cracks in it and the walls were block with a door to what looked like a tunnel.

This place was awesome, it even had a closed circuit tv for cameras out front and all around the house. As I closed the trap door the couch moved back on it's own and the rug had a pull cord that was on the underside of it. It was so thin I barely saw it when Julia grabbed it and pulled the rug back in place.

"We can stay here for now, and if they find the door we can exit through the tunnel. The tunnel is actually a maze that will certainly get them lost and if they don't keep track of where they go, they will die in it. Don't worry, I know the way through and it comes out a little over a mile down the mountain and we have a vehicle there just for the purpose of making a get away." She said softly with a sly grin on her face.

We stood there watching on the screen as Gene and the biker guy was trying to sneak up to the house, kind of laughing to ourselves the closer they got. Just as Gene was about to hit the tripwire for the claymore, the biker stopped him.

He made Gene step back a few yards and he grabbed a good sized piece of wood, I didn't have to see what he was going to do, I knew! He checked the fallen limb from a tree onto the wire and BOOM! The claymore went off just like it was suppose to do, except it didn't quite serve it's purpose.

The two of them slowly and very cautiously eased up on the porch and started looking through the windows. The biker after looking through a couple of them turned the knob and eased the door open. They both walked in the door one after the other and started looking around. Gene of course started looking for anything that would show we were there but, the biker started looking for ways out of the place.

The biker started kind of stomping the floor. "What the hell are you doing? Are you insane, they will know we are here for sure now!" Gene whispered angrily.

"If there is a trap door or false floor, it will make a different sound, dumb ass!" the biker smarter off.

At the moment he started stomping I motioned for Julia to follow me. We quietly made our way to the door to the tunnel and slowly opened the door. Surprisingly it didn't squeak or make any sound what so ever. I didn't want to take the chance of them finding the trap door and us having to make a hasty get away, so we needed to go right then.

Once in the tunnel there was another door that blended in with the surroundings. Once we were through this door and shut it lights came on in the tunnel, and I could see what she meant about it being a maze. It literally looked as if someone had made a maze straight from Greek mythology. There were different ways to go but, Julia knew which path to take. To seemed like we had been walking for a good fifteen minutes and all of a sudden the lights went out.

"They found the door!" Julia whispered.

Just as she said this the lights came back on. We walked on certain it would be safe to go on. After walking another few minutes we came to another door I reached to open it and she grabbed my hand and shook her head to say no. She then pointed to a wall and pushed a stone on it and another door opened quietly. We hurried through the door and shut it behind us.

"That was a trap that would have kept us in there until someone came into the maze to save us. This way is more tunnels, just not as confusing as the maze was." She said with a little grin.

"Good thing you were quick enough to catch me before I turned the handle to open that door! Although shouldn't we be quieter so they don't hear us?" I said kind of concerned.

"Nope, the wall we just came through makes this side sound proof . It is made that way so you can't hear nature or anything else to help you find your way out." Julia sheepishly said.

As we walked on through the tunnels I began to see light coming from the end of the one we were in and she told me the garage was just up ahead. As we walked into the garage I saw a red light on the wall adjacent to the one we came out of the tunnel from. When I asked what that was she simply said "Those two will never see the light of day again!" and at that moment I knew what they had done. They had found the door I almost tried to open.

There was a tarp covering what seemed to be some sort of vehicle. After removing the tarp I saw it was a all terrain vehicle kind of like a golf cart with 4 wheel drive. She hopped On it and started it.

"I have to go back, we can't take any chances that they will get out of there! I also need to get Mimi!" I demanded.

She assured me they weren't going to get out when...

BOOM!

They must have found the explosives that were left over and used them to blow a hole in the wall. I could hear Gene say "They had to go this way!" and I knew this had to end here and now.

Chapter Six: A horrid escape

   I told her to go on and leave me one of my rifles and my Ka-Bar knife. Reluctantly she did as I asked. She took off and I settled down behind a low lying box and waited what seemed to be an eternity. I began to see shadows but I wanted to make sure I got a clear shot, so I waited until I saw them both. They had gotten smarter, because they had on ballistics jackets. This was going to be difficult was all I could think. Then I remembered a story my uncle had told me of a shot he took. He shot one guy who was running in the head because he had a flak jacket on he had taken from an American soldier. I knew I only had one try at this because after my first shot they would start shooting up the place.

   I squeezed the trigger just as I was taught and in between inhaling and exhaling I finished the squeeze. The bullet tore right through one of their heads like it was a watermelon. The other had leaned slightly to the left and the bullet ripped through the top part of his shoulder. This was a lucky shot, because I kind of got a two for one.

I could hear the other guy scream in pain then let out a few obscenities. That gave me enough time to roll over and come up to a crouching position beside the doorway. I stayed there for what seemed to be an eternity. The one that came out was the biker and he was still armed and searching the room. As he walked by me I jumped up and with one fatal swoop I wrapped my arm around his neck and drove my Ka-Bar up through his kidney and on into his ribcage hoping to hit his heart.

He gasped and tried to break free but, all he could do was grab at me and try to hit me. After a few seconds he started to slump and I dropped his lifeless body to the floor. I made my way to outside and started walking up the hill.

I hoped that Julia made it safely to the cabin as I slowly made my way up the hill. I got closer to the top and I could see the shack and the carport where Mimi was. I did not see Julia though and I did not see the vehicle she had.

I began to look around to see if there was any sign of Julia being at the cabin and leaving but, I saw nothing. I decided to go to in and get a few things to take with me and try to find other things I could use as a weapon. I did find a baseball bat and an axe outside in the garage, I also found a sledgehammer with the handle cut off to where it was only about a foot long. I took the axe but, didn't take the sledgehammer.

Once I loaded everything into the truck and started it up, I backed out and started to go down the road. At that moment I realized I had forgotten one thing. The booby trap we had set on the road. I stopped the truck and cut it off. When I grabbed the axe and my pistol, I wondered if I would need anything else. It would take my knife too.

I grabbed the knife and shoved it down the back of my pants and put the pistol down the front. I started the hike down the hill to the trap and hoped I would run into Julia on the way. The walk was kind of difficult all because the road was mainly dirt and big rock. This made it slippery because of moisture that had gathered on the rocks. I slowly walked to the trap as I got closer.

I tried stepping in between the rocks and on the dirt but, sometimes it wasn't possible. Once I got to the trap I remembered that the tripwire was across a huge rock. I inched my way down to it on the side of the explosives. The worst thing ever happened as I got to the trigger for the trap, my foot slipped and I slid down the face of the rock. One leg went over the tripwire but, the other went under it. Luckily neither of them set it off and double luck because, the explosives were right in front of my face.

I carefully unhooked a battery I had rigged up to set off the explosives and put a piece of wood in between the connectors for the trigger. I slowly moved the explosives to where the tripwire was loose and moved my legs. I then took the detonator out of the dynamite and stuck it in my pocket. The dynamite of course might come in handy. At that exact moment I heard a commotion down below where I was.

It seemed to be coming from the area where the deep rut was. I could make out one voice as being Julia's but, the other was a man I didn't recognize...

...at first.

The second voice once I got a little closer I recognized as Chuck, the pastor at YOU. He was arguing with Julia telling her she would regret killing the biker and her ex. I didn't remember us killing her ex but, then I thought about the one biker and Gene walking up to the cabin after the explosion in the woods.

They were covered in blood splatter. That must have been from her ex, he must have came with them to show where the cabin was. All I could think about after that was getting Julia away from him. I inched my way toward where they were and the closer I got the lower I got until I was actually crawling .

I got close enough to try to get him with the pistol, when I feel a tap on my foot. It was another member of the church! The only thing I could think of then was, ah crap! I stood up and he walked me to where Julia and Chuck were. When I got closer Chuck smarts off saying "So this is what we get for being relaxed but, nice of you to drop by Brandon!"

"I was explaining to your girlfriend here, she took several of my members from me and the head church doesn't like that. We now have to take you guys to one of the other churches and let them deal with you. They don't seem too happy with the way I am taking care of things so they are sending a cleaner team to clean up the mess you guys have made around town. My cleaner team of course is no longer living thanks to you two!" Chuck said hatefully.

There was no way I was going to let them take me anywhere. I felt a sharp pain in the back of my head and the next thing I knew I was waking up in a small room with Julia there crying and whispering "Are you ok?"

"of course I am, it will take a lot more than a hit and to the back of my head to damage me."

Which was a bold faced lie. My head felt as if they had been drilling in it for days and throbbed like a toothache. I couldn't let her think I was too weak to handle their brute force tactics. I had to hold it together and think of a way out of this.

I noticed Julia was handcuffed to a bar that was shackled to her ankles and was basically hogtied. Mine were not as bad I was handcuffed to a metal handle on the wall and I noticed the floor was ceramic tile. They had us in a bathroom somewhere! I looked around to see if I could use anything to unlock the cuffs. Then I remembered I had a paper clip that I had put in my pocket at work the last time I was there.

   I managed to get my hips high enough to reach one hand into my pocket and pull it out. I straightened it as best I could and started trying to unlock the cuffs.

   I almost had it when a guy walked in. I hid the paper clip in my hand the only way I could. The guy walks over to Julia and grabs her arms lifting her off the floor just enough to carry her out of the room screaming to the top of her lungs to stop. He did but, only to kick her in the head and tell her to shut up. He picked her back up and carried her out of the room shutting the door behind him. I didn't here any lock so that was a plus.

   I started back trying to unlock the cuffs. Finally I caught the latch and pulled on the cuffs, they sprang open and rattled on the metal pipe. I hurried and unlocked the other one and went to the door. I slowly opened it so I could see at least the one way outside. We were in some sort of park. I don't know where but I did recognize a couple of things and noticed they had Julia handcuffed to a tree now with the bar still attached to her ankles. They were trying to get her to tell them where the information was that she had found.

  She was a real trooper, because she wasn't telling them anything at all. I shut the door to see what I could find as a weapon and the only thing I found was a plunger. That would have to do for right now. I pulled the cup off the end of the handle. I shoved the handle in the metal hand hold I was handcuffed to and broke the wooden handle on an angle to make a sort of spear. I then checked out the window to see if it was big enough for me to get through. Sure enough it was just big enough, the problem was getting up to it.

  I managed to climb up and out of the window, sliding down the side of the block building. It felt like I was using a whet stone on my body. I checked around the side of the building to see if anyone else was around and there wasn't. I went out into the woods behind the bathroom and then realized the had taken me to Flag Rock camping area and there was an old logging road below where we were that would lead back around behind them. I managed to get to it and I heard the guys say "He escaped!" and another one say to find me.

I heard one of them coming toward me and I hid in a big mountain laurel bush. I saw him walk in front of the Bush and I leapt out onto his legs and drove the plunger handle through his back and up into his heart. I could feel the stick go past his diaphragm and into the meat of his heart with a grinding like slide.

I held my arm against the back of his head as to keep his scream from being heard by the others. His life force draining into the burnt orange, brown, and red leaves, running a small crimson river down the hill. When he finally quit moving, I stood up and drug his body to the laurel bush and covered it with as many leaves as I could. I then covered the blood on the path as best I could. I also retrieved my knife from his belt and took his pistol from the holster.

I heard another of them up above me but, he didn't seem to be coming my way. Easing up the trail, walking toe to heal I crept along until I got around to where Julia was. I crouched down behind a table that a limb from a tree had lodged against and watched them. I had to think of something to get her free and I knew there were only three more of them. An idea came to mind from a lot of shows and movies I had seen before. Picking up a couple of rocks I threw one over away from me and to where the lone man would have to walk by where I was to check it out.

He did just like I thought he would, waiting for him to walk closer hiding behind the dead leaves of the tree branch quietly. He got just on the other side of the table and I jumped out and stabbed him down through his collarbone into his artery while holding my hand over his mouth. I could feel the knife scrape his bone and the muscle pop as the knife went through it. A steady stream of blood ran down his body onto the ground. He slumped onto the bench attached to the table. Once he did that I pulled the knife out and sat him up against a tree near the table.

After assuring he was going to stay upright, I quietly walked over to Julia and got her cuffs off with a key I found on the guy I had just killed. She hugged me like she never had before. Before any of the others came back, we needed to head for the main gate. So I rushed her hug and told her we needed to hurry.

As we were walking toward the main gate I saw one of the men walking towards us but through the trees and he hadn't noticed us yet. The first thing I did was grab a rock and throw it into the woods to draw his attention away from us. While he was searching the foliage I got Julia to lay down beside the paved road and I did the same in front of her. Pulling the pistol out I had, I aimed it right for him but waited until he got a little closer. When he got close enough I squeezed the trigger and hit him right in the chest with the bullet.

I knew the last guy would come our way because of the shot, so I helped Julia up and walked over to the guy and made sure he was dead. He had a faint pulse so I used my knife and finished him. I searched his pockets for keys and found two sets. One was what looked like keys for a building and the other was for a GM vehicle and a Dodge vehicle. I just took the vehicle keys and hurried Julia along to the gate which was only about a hundred yards away from where we were.

Once we reached the gate I saw the vehicles that were there and one was a GM and the other a Ford. I got Julia in the passenger seat and got into the driver side of the Equinox and luckily the key was the right one. The GM came to life as I turned the key. The other guy came running around the curve pulling his gun out as he did. Without thinking I pulled my pistol and shot the tires on the other vehicle.

He started shooting at us as I started backing around. I had thought this would happen, so I had backed around behind the other vehicle to keep something in between us and him. As I pulled forward the sign for Flag Rock blocked his shots also, at least until I pulled out up the hill. A few shots came through the back of the vehicle but, nothing hit us. I got to the top of the hill and turned down towards the recreation lake. I took all the roads to come out on the Tacoma side of high knob.

I happened to think of a cousin who lived around there and I stopped in to ask if they knew anywhere we could hide out for a few days until the stuff blew over. He mentioned one place he knew of but, it was on the other side of Norton and would take about forty five minutes to get to it from the road and that was walking in. He had the key to a shack that had heat, food, and running water in it for hunting. The bad part was that he didn't have a key for the gate at the bottom.

Chapter Seven: The new, new hideout

I wasn't going to look a gift horse in the mouth, so I took that. He offered to let me clean up there, but I turned it down and he mentioned the place had an outside shower with it but the water was gas heated. I opted for the other shower which is what would be best so I could wash my clothes out while I showered.

I took the key and a hunting rifle he offered to the vehicle and told Julia of the place and she agreed it would be better to do that. The only thing is I had to figure out where to park and we would have to walk from there. The drive there was tense but quiet. Once we reached where the gate was I let Julia out with the rifle and a few other items I thought we might need and drove back down near highway 23. Once I got there it was about 11:30 at night and I had an idea to cover where we were.

I decided to put a board I had found on the gas and aim the car toward the rock high wall across the road. Once I fastened the steering wheel as stable as I could, I put the car in Drive and jumped out. The car hit the wall at about 40 mph and flipped on its roof. It skidded out the wall and rolled over and over until it hit the guardrail and over it the car jumped.

   A few seconds later it caught fire and it could be seen for a long distance because it was a fairly clear night. Once I saw the bright orange-yellow glow, I started walking to the gate. It took about eight to ten minutes to reach where the gate was and once I did I saw Julia sitting against a tree. Once we met up, we began the long walk up the old rugged dirt road.

   The road looked as if no one had traveled it in years and was riddled with ruts and holes, with the occasional rock sticking out. It was a grueling trek up the hill and took us about twenty five to thirty minutes but, seemed to be hours. Once we reached the shack of my cousins, Julia asked what the fire she could see below was and I explained what I had done with the car.

She kind of understood why I did it but, also couldn't figure out how we were going to be get somewhere without a car. I explained that we would just call a cousin to have them drop supplies down the hill in different places in lock boxes and we'd get them. This seemed to satisfy her question as an answer.

We had been through so much in the last few days and we didn't know if tomorrow would bring an end to the madness by either them stopping or us dying. All I knew is that I was tired physically and emotionally. What seemed like a walk to the shack being forever I still enjoyed it, because it was with Julia. I needed to just think for a few minutes, but I had too much to do.

What I really wanted to do was shower but, I let her shower first and I took a walk and was watching the EMS teams search the crash site. I must have been more tired than I thought because I fell asleep leaning against a tree.

Chapter Eight: now that were all caught up!

Looking at my hands the morning dew had made the blood from the previous day wet again and was dripping down onto the leaves below them. I wish everything could have went different is all I could think. Too many lives were lost for the silly religion that was suppose to be so peaceful and serene.

I still couldn't wrap my mind around the fact that a religion could be so violent and persecute any non believers.

Just at that moment Julia comes up behind me. "I was wondering where you went to. At least now you'll probably have a warmer shower than I did." Julia stated

After having an in depth conversation about next to nothing and about how I had to just vedge out, to kind of detach from the moment. She understood completely, because she had done the same thing in the shower.

Brandon gets up and goes to wrap his arm around Julia.

"Not until you take a shower mister! I just got all that gunk off me and after the last few days, I want to stay clean ...at least for a little while." Julia says jerking away.

After we got back to the shack, I went to grab some clothes from the closet there and Julia motioned toward the bed. "I already have clothes out for you, just get in the shower and I'll bring them to you!"

She was getting a little bossy now and I guess it was from us almost dying a few times in the last few days. It was ok though I kind of liked it, which was a little unusual for me.

I went out and got into the shower and after I finally got all the blood cleaned off me and the rest of my body washed, I heard Julia coming out of the shack and lay my clothes on the small bench just outside the shower under the awning that covered both. The odd thing was I also heard her put other things down after the Initial sound of clothing. The next thing I know, the door to the shower opens and she steps in.

"Wh wh what are you doing?" I managed to stutter the words.

Julia's reply was just a big grin and a "Just helping you clean up."

She took the rag and started washing my back. "I notice you don't seem to mind this. As a matter of fact it looks as if you like it a lot!" Julia says looking around me.

She slowly moves the rag around my hips and begins to wash me in ways I had never had done. She gently caressed me and before I knew it she was kissing on my neck. The night after the shower was just awesome, that is all I want to say about it.

A couple of hours later we were lying in the twin sized bed when she just blurted out. "Why the hell haven't I went for you before now. Considering we are running for our lives and may not see the end of the week! Damn it, we could have had something wonderful!"

I just rolled over and kissed her and brushed her hair while saying "I know how we can get those goons off our backs. We make a deal, to quote Scarface, one they can't refuse!"

Julia looked puzzled "And what would that be pray tell?"

I began to tell her about an idea I had of us making them leave us alone and us not having to constantly run and hide from them. After going through everything I had to make a phone call to a friend who would in turn set up the meeting. They would also insure we wouldn't be harmed.

See this friend of mine Dave, was a Marine and not just any old Marine, he was a Scout Sniper in the Marines. He not only still was an expert marksman, he was still a certified sniper trainer and trained the best of the civilian police.

I called him and explained my idea to him and after a debate over the method of security I had come up with, he agreed to go with my plan.

See I had the idea to meet them where they had no way of surprising us with a bunch of goons to capture anyone. The whole thing hinged on my friend Brett. He would have them meet us at the parking lot of the local fairgrounds. This would give us an advantage.

It means he can stay a half a mile away and still keep us safe. He also had a buddy of his that he could trust he could get to help cover us. All this was decided by him in just a matter of seconds after I told him what had been going on.

He called me back after a few hours to tell me we were on for 2 days from then at 3pm that day. He also wanted to let me know that he had a few surprises for them as well.

When I told Julia about this she got really anxious and almost relieved.

CHAPTER NINE :The best non-option

The day of the meeting Julia and I decided to stop by and get something to eat on our way to the meeting. We didn't want to do this on an empty stomach. We decided on Western Steer and a steak meal. Dave didn't like the idea, but he didn't have a say so in the matter.

We ordered our meal and sat down in the back room for privacy. The manager tried to talk us into sitting in the front area, but we insisted. It seemed as if the order took forever and ever to get to us. When it only took a few minutes.

I had ordered the biggest ribeye they had medium rare and a baked potato and fried. Julia ordered a sirloin and fried. Dave just got the buffet bar and mainly ate salad, which we had a salad along with our meal too.

I don't know if it was because of us not eating this kind of food for so long or that we were about to face people who wanted to kill us. This was the best steak I had ever eaten and the potatoes were perfect.

As we both finished, Dave started trying to rush us out of there. We finished our food and started walking toward the door when Dave told us to hide. They had found us and weren't going to wait for the meeting.

What they didn't count on was us knowing the manager, who unlocked the alarm on the back door and let us out and set the alarm back. When the guys went into the back room we made our way out front and drove off.

On the way to the fairgrounds I told Dave to drop Julia off at a cousins house close to there and she started saying "We are in this together and I am going too, no argument!"

I tried to reason with her, but she wouldn't accept anything but going with me. This was not a good idea because, if I were to be taken by them and she was safe, then she could send the information to the state police to show what was going on. With her being there, well that leaves no one to tell the story.

Well no one but Dave, and he doesn't know all of it. In or order to catch him up on the details, I gave him the abridged version ...and gave him the flash drive all the documents I had on it. Of course I had also given a drive just like it to another friend a few weeks back too.

Redundancy is a good thing sometimes! Now to our destined meeting.

The plan was to drop Dave off a short distance away from the rendezvous point...and give him enough time to get set up. Then we would pull out and continue to the fairgrounds to wait.

We reached the drop-off point and he took off running up the hill. We heard a little commotion in the leaves and I assumed he had tripped. My phone rang and it was Dave letting me know he was ready but, to wait a few minutes to get out of his hummer so he could check the area. When I asked him why he explained that the commotion was a sniper waiting for us. He wanted to make sure no others were out there besides his crew.

Considering the situation I wasn't going to argue. After the call, I pulled out toward our destined rendezvous. Once we arrived I did as Dave had suggested and sat there in the vehicle.

There was a black Escalade pulled up to the front of the Hummer and all of a sudden there was a thud on the windshield as if a rock had hit it. Then a shot rang out from behind us. There was a man right after that fell from the high h wall in front of us. The phone vibrated as it rang again. It was Dave letting us know the coast was clear. He kind of laughed a little when he said: "Aren't you glad I installed the bulletproof glass?" Of course, the answer was yes!

With the call, of course, we got out of the Hummer and started to walk toward the Escalade. As we did the leader of YOU for the area got out and so did another man. Chuck (the leader), introduced us...

"This is Lee, the regional minister for the church, and this is Lynn his assistant. She is here to take notes and draw up an agreement." Chuck exclaimed as a woman got out of the back.

"I am going to start by saying, if we don't leave here or anything happens to us all the major networks will get the information I have gathered! I also have a few back up contingencies to make sure we get out of here alive! The next thing I want to say is that we want to be left alone and live our lives like we were before all of this! This means no threats and no having to look over our shoulders for the rest of our lives. That is the beginning of what we want...after you accept these we will continue and you can let us know what you would like." I said nervously.

Chuck shook his head in agreement but, Lee didn't like the idea and started arguing with Chuck. Not only did he argue with him but, pulled a pistol saying "I have the solution right here and I will take matters into my own hands!"

At that moment another shot rang out and blood splattered all over their vehicle and the Hummer, as well as us. I opened my eyes back up to see Lee holding his hand, or what was left of it in his other hand. He was screaming so loud he could have woke the dead.

I wanted to say sorry but, what came out was not so nice. "I told you, you stupid asshole! We came loaded for bear and you came loaded for pheasant!" I shouted.

His assistant shouted "You're the asshole, all he was doing was going to get rid of Chuck! He is the one doing all of this!"

"I'm sorry, but the last few weeks have been very, very hectic and bloody. The two goons that leave dead bodies with Greek symbols on them in their wake made sure of that. I took care of them though and more took their place." I smarted off.

She didn't say a word after that but, Lee struggling muttered "And you have your wish, you can live your lives especially since it seems you are smarter than we are and can take care of yourselves."

As I look around at Chuck, Lynn runs to the side of the Escalade and grabs a hunting rifle. She has a military grade starlight and infrared scope on it. I motioned for Julia to get into the vehicle and turned to get in myself. Lynn laid down behind the Escalade to hide, she knew what direction it had come from. Dave knows how to take care of himself and knows what to do in cases like this.

Just as I go to get in Chuck grabs me by the shoulder and I pulled the Glock strapped to the inside of the door. I put the pistol on his nose and told him to back off. Chuck nervously "Please don't leave me! I am not the one who has been doing all of this, I am just the pastor of the church and have never wanted any part of the deaths! Lynn had sent the thugs and ordered the deaths of all those people! Please help me!"

I felt Julia's hand on my other shoulder and heard as she said "He's telling the truth, let's go!"

I got in and Chuck hopped in the back. Even though I was pulling out Lynn was still obsessed with searching for the one who shot Lee and didn't notice us. There was another shot from in front of us and I saw blood splatter on the windshield. When I used the wipers I saw Lynn holding her leg and could hear her scream over the sound of the engine.

I wasn't stopping to see if we had reached an agreement or not with Lee. Chuck from the back seat started yelling: "Let's get out of here before the rest get here!"

I raced out of the dirt and gravel parking lot throwing some gravel on the way out. I hurried down to where we dropped Dave off and of course, where he was waiting for us. He opened the back door and immediately drew his gun.

"Don't worry, dude he is on our side," I reassured him.

"Since when?" Dave exclaimed.

Julia with certainty "Since the very beginning. Just get in and we'll explain."

Dave gets in and as he does he starts demanding to know what is going on. The whole time he doesn't take his gun off of Chuck.

"Take it easy Dave, holster your cannon (because he carried a .50 caliber Desert Eagle) and just calm down some!" came out of my mouth. He did just that but, took the holster off before he did and laid it away from Chuck.

"Ok chuck, let's hear it...why should we trust you!?" Dave commanded.

Chuck began to explain that he was just a pawn in the whole church and that Lynn was a lunatic fanatic. She would do anything to see the church rise to international levels and become the next big thing.

CHAPTER TEN: And The Story Goes On

After explaining the whole story of how he wanted to be a pastor and liked the idea of the YOU church, he jumped at the chance to preach. Even though he had on numerous occasions showed a blatant disagreement with Lynn and Lee over how to handle those who disagreed with them. This put him at risk of being dealt with himself if he hadn't of been such a charismatic speaker he would have been just another statistic.

He was lucky in that sense but, he had to put on a front with them as to not be discovered. The whole time they were ordering people killed he would misplace the letters sent to him about others. This raised some questions which caused the two bikers to be sent in to take over for "PR" reasons.

    They were the ones who came up with the idea to brand each and every victim with a Greek symbol of the god, goddess, or mythological person on them which described what they were killed for. This Chuck really didn't like and said he voiced his opinion on the matter but, nothing he said would change their mind. See the two bikers okayed the idea with Lynn and she thought it was just suiting for those who would betray the faith or reveal any lie about it.

    Those two had cleaned up messes in several states and never been bested by anyone, until Brandon. Chuck said that he had made them really want to get him out of the way and that is why they had went after Julia. Gene had told them of the strong friendship they had and that going after her would flush him out.

    The worst thing was that they had planned on holding her and messaging him to get him to come to them. Of course as you know this backfired on them.

"Julia, how did you know Chuck wasn't behind all of this and wasn't just trying to get us to take him as to save his own life?" I asked.

"That answer is easy. Chuck is my half brother and he had given me some of the information I had. Also he was telling me more stuff when you were captured at the cabin." Julia responded.

Brandon almost ran out of the road when she said this. Dave asked him to pull over and let him drive but, Brandon refused.

Chuck continued to tell about several different times he had seen the bikers at other YOU congregations and why. He told of one in Pennsylvania they had killed around fifteen to twenty people and had to move on to somewhere else to keep from being found out. Then they would go to another town and do the same and return months later to finish the "work" they had started.

The trail of blood and bodies that followed them was numerous and horrific, to say the least. They were too good at their job most of the time. One place they even had given a man a viral infection that spread to his whole family and on his deathbed had branded him with a symbol of pestilence.

Then one they used the symbol for Hades and set the house on fire while he was sleeping with a cigar laying on his pillow because he smoked cigars. Another they had used Neptune and drown the man with his fishing vest on holding his fishing pole. There were too many to name but, Chuck could go on for days with deaths the two were responsible for.

After all the information he had given, Dave decided to call in a few favors from old military buddies.

CHAPTER ELEVEN: The little war in Wise County

Dave was certain he needed help with protecting us. He had me go to a remote location out in the Pumpkin gap area. We pulled up to a chain link gate that leads into a field, where he got out and walked up to the gate. He had a walking stick that he pushed into the ground and a keypad came up.

He turned and told us not to look and entered a code. I know he did because I heard the tones from the entries. He got back into the Hummer and just said "drive."

I started driving down this little path of a road which seemed to appear from nowhere. The gate closed behind us after we drove through it. It the was just like a self-storage complex but without the buildings. After driving for what seemed to be forever, we came upon a mound with a door in it.

It looked as if it couldn't be big enough for maybe two or three people to be in it at a time. He just said, "we're here!" and once we stopped he got out.

Once again he asked us to not look and I heard a mechanical whir from his direction and the beeps of a keypad. After the beeps, he grabs my shoulder and turns me around. I tell the others to come on and we walk inside.

There are steps going down what looks like for a hundred yards or so. We get halfway down them and there is a curtain, it is a painting of steps going on down. This is awesome, because, the curtain is hiding what looks like a 5-star hotel suite. There is a bar fully stocked to the right side as you go in, a kitchen just past that, what looks like a seventy-inch television on the wall to the left with just about every game console you could want, and three doors leading out of that area that is toward the back of the room. Right in the middle of the room is a huge sectional couch that wraps around a big black shag rug and behind that is a huge oval table with a big bulldog wearing a Smokey bear hat.

If I didn't know any better I'd say this was Dave's man cave.

Dave handed me a key fob from a hook on the wall "If you have to leave, this will get you back in and also will open the door to your room. There are only three rooms but, I don't think you and Julia will have a problem sharing huh?"

I asked about a shower and a change of clothes and he told me there was a shower in my room and a change of clothes for both of us. I started to ask him why he had women's clothing but, I really didn't want to know.

I opened the door to the room Dave said was mine and as I walked in I motioned for Julia to follow me. Julia immediately followed me into the room. As I shut the door Dave said: "Oh and by the way, it's soundproof." Jokingly and laughed.

Julia and I showered together and got into bed without getting dressed. After all why would we get dressed, if we were going to just take it off?

In the middle of the night I heard a commotion and then gunfire. I peeked out of the door to find Dave and Chuck playing a war-game on the Xbox. I got dressed and went out to join them. As I walked out, I smelled something wonderful to eat. It was like Chinese food and Italian mixed. I looked over to the kitchen and saw two others there.

One was John, an old buddy of Dave and I that was an ex-Navy Seal and the other was a guy I had seen with Dave before. The other guy was Juan and was an ex-seal also and seeing them there I knew Dave had something planned.

Dave noticed me walking out and smirked saying "Did you have fun?"

"Oh, shut it smartass!" I snapped at him.

They all laughed at my comment and just went back to what they were doing. Julia must have caught a whiff of the food because she came out of the room a few minutes after I did. She walked up to me and hugged me tight and whispered: "Don't you ever leave me!"

"Never!" was my response.

We sat down at the table and Juan walked over with two plates of food that smelled divine. We ate like we hadn't eaten in weeks. Come to think of it we really hadn't eaten much for a couple of weeks.

After we ate Dave paused the game and switched the channel on the tv to what looked like plans. Dave had been busy planning something but, what I was about to find out.

He started telling what he had planned while we were asleep was a raid on the regional office and a promise to Lynn and Lee of what we would do. When I asked what he needed those two for he just said "It's better you don't know why!"

"Is Chuck, Julia, and myself going with you?" was my next question for him. He just shook his head no and said: "You guys are staying right here, do not leave no matter what!"

They got ready to leave and Dave walked over to the wall beside the tv and waved his hand to a tiny almost invisible camera in the wall. The wall started moving with a mechanical whir to reveal several weapons on special hangers. He then reached for an old M-14 and handed it to me.

"If I'm not going what do I need this for?" I asked.

"Follow me and I will show you exactly what that is for!" Dave responded.

When I followed him he took me to a small room just inside the corner of the kitchen. I thought it was a cupboard but, it had a ladder leading straight up. He motioned for me to climb up it and I did just that. Once I reached the top I looked around and it was a little turret that swiveled 360° and had a small hole in it that the barrel of the M-14 fit in perfectly.

Then I hear from just below me, "Sweet isn't it? You don't have to worry about aiming either...push the little button right beside of the gun hole."

When I did a small twelve-inch screen lit up and every time the turret swiveled it moved around and when I moved the rifle, the scene moved. It was a type of tracking camera used as a scope for the rifle. Looked like he had about every kind of gadget you could come up with here to ward off intruders.

When I reached the bottom of the ladder, Dave motioned for me to follow him again. I did and when we got back in front of the tv he picked the remote up and as he changed the input I saw the gate. The cameras changed though, from the gate to the top of the mound, to satellite, to different areas around the mound.

"You don't have to sit here and watch this either. There are sensors that trip and will bring the camera up that is near that area. That way you don't have to be bored." Dave explained.

At that moment the tv switched to the gate and a red light started flashing. "That idiot forgot his old keys again. Don't worry Brandon, it is just an old buddy of ours. You know him as Jack, we know him as 'Ripper'." Dave said.

The three of them went up the steps to meet Jack at the door. All but Dave were dressed in some sort of camp and combat boots.

I hurried to the ladder to see what was going on, only to see all, including Jack, get into the Hummer. At that moment my phone rang, it was Dave "Man get down off the ladder and go to the first kitchen cabinet you come to."

I shimmied down the ladder and opened the cabinet to find a military style communication radio. When I turned it on I here Dave again telling me to push a button on it. He then explains that the button is to encrypt the signal so we can talk and not be understood. He also explains that Chuck had given him a few coordinates to strategic places to cripple the church and their ability to track us.

He also explained there would be silence on here until they are returning to the bunker. Then there was definitely silence on it.

A few hours went by and nothing on the radio and no calls on my phone and I was starting to get worried that something had gone wrong and they weren't successful.

   The tv switched to a camera at the gate and no alarm. The gate opened and it was the Hummer. I could see in the video feed it had a few scratches from what looked like bullets hitting it. Just in case I grabbed the M-14 and scurried up the ladder and stuck the barrel in the gun hoke, then turned the screen on. I waited for them to come into sight and aimed the rifle at one of the windows on the Hummer. I waited and it stopped, the doors flew open, and the foursome got out.

   Then Jack turned back around and drug a person out with a black bag over their head and an orange jumpsuit on. The person moved like a woman, I kept thinking no it can't be.

   The for of them came in the door and down the steps with the person. Straight to the back room, they went and Dave motioned for me to follow him, which I did.

CHAPTER TWELVE: The interrogation

Once we got into the back room, the guys put the person in a metal chair toward the back of the room. They proceeded in tying the person to it and making sure there was plenty enough room to walk behind them.

The other two went into a closet and got out three big lights that looked as if they would melt your skin off if you stayed in their light too long. They placed them around the front of the chair about two or three feet in front of it.

Once they had everything just right they cut the main light off and turned the three sun lamps on. Juan took a bottle of water and poured it over the persons head. It soaked the bag and the person coughed and choked on the water. "No matter what torture you do, I am not going to crack and give in!" a woman's voice said.

Juan took the hood off and it was Lynn. They had captured her to get her to yield to what they wanted. It didn't look like that would work either. Dave began talking "Why do you have to kill those who oppose you and think differently? Can't you just let them be and let them believe what they want? Then again if you never make it out of here, this killing will end!"

"We don't HAVE to kill all who oppose us! Just the radical ones! Like you gentlemen!" Lynn shouted

"Our friends aren't radicals and you have tried to kill them! They just were finding out information and hadn't even tied it all to you or Lee, or for that matter anyone but the two thugs you hired, but you tried to kill them and us!" Dave stated in a drill instructor like voice.

"What do you want from me then? I mean I am not going to kill them after all, Lee made an agreement with them to let them go!" Lynn shouted.

"We just want all of us to be left alone and let us live our lives in peace! Is that too much to ask?" came out before I could stop myself.

"Of course that can be arranged and I am not just saying that either. Let me go and I will make sure that happens, just as long as nothing makes it to the news about what is going on." Lynn says reluctantly.

"How do we know you aren't going to just say that and as soon as they show up in public, boom you snatch them up and kill them, huh?" Dave asks.

"You don't, you just have to take me at my word and if I don't then I guess I will meet my maker," Lynn says sheepishly.

"You've got that right lady! We will be YOUR judge, jury, and executioners!" Jack smarts off.

The guys motion for me to leave the room and when they do I ask why. Their response was simply, "You don't want to see this!"

I reluctantly left the room and when I did, Julia was standing there waiting for me. The first thing she did was ask me who it was they had. When I told her what they had done and that I didn't know what they were doing, she shook her head and said, "Oh god, what have we gotten into?"

Chuck, of course, was just playing a game when the screen suddenly went to showing the gate and an SUV at it.

I opened the door to the back room again and told them we have company. As soon as I did the red lights started flashing again and they covered Lynn's head up. She was halfway laughing and crying for some reason and said, "They are coming for me, assholes!"

"Brandon get to the turret, and guys follow me!" Dave said.

Of course, I rushed to the turret and the other guys ran up the stairs and out the door. When I turned the screen on I saw them with Ghillie suits getting ready to hide.

Julia came to the ladder and asked what can she do and I told her to guard the back room. She rushed out and I heard her chamber a bullet in a pistol.

I turned my attention to the screen and watched as the SUV got closer and closer. It pulled right beside of the Hummer and out of sight for me to take a shot. This was solved after two of them stepped out and towards the door. I waited until I saw one of them run back around to the side and I took the shot for the lone guy. I didn't aim at his head but aimed at his left thigh instead to wound him.

I could see him rolling on the ground in agony but, I couldn't hear him. At least until one of our guys opened the door and I could hear him screaming then I heard a thud and no more screaming. Jack, Juan, and Dave had subdued the others and were bringing them inside to talk to them. John was carrying the wounded man who he took to the backroom and the others followed with the prisoners. Dave stuck his head out and motioned for me to cone on in to the room. I took Julia by the hand and started walking to the room but, Dave shook his head no. "She doesn't go. then I don't go!" came out before I could think.

Dave just motioned for us to come on in at that point and we walked in hand in hand. Once we got in there we saw the guy I had shot lying on the bed unconscious. Juan handed me a med kit and said, "Do your worst."

Julia and I proceeded to bandage him up. Good thing I had shot his left leg instead of his left or he would be lying outside dead from blood loss. I also had shot through his femur which would have needed surgery if I hadn't of used an fmj (full metal jacket for those laymen) but, it just had a hole straight through it. I used a pack and a half of gauze in the wound and packed it tight to slow the bleeding. As soon as I finished packing the wound Julia had the bandages ready with some betadine on the wound side. I taped it up and made sure he had enough tape to keep it from coming off when he moves. By that time the guys had secured the others to chairs and on the floor.

The fun for Juan, Jack, John, and Dave had just begun. The foursome started to interrogate the crew and it wasn't pretty. Juan drug one into the bathroom and over to the shower. Juan grabs a towel and lays the guy on the floor of the shower and places the towel over his face. He then pulls the shower head own stretching the hose for it toward the guy and turns the water on. After only a few minutes the guy begins to talk incessantly, even though the other two that were awake kept insisting he shut up.

They had been sent in by Lee to get Lynn back and they weren't the only crew out. They were in fact the only crew trained in any sort of combat. The other guys were just a bunch of "rednecks with guns and of no threat to us and our bunker." He said.

CHAPTER THIRTEEN: The Sunday Sermons

After finding out what thy knew the foursome talked to Lynn who, reluctantly agreed to let us be left alone and live our lives in peace. Only if we joined the church and kept quiet about the killings and the killings would stop. Of course we agreed to the terms but, only if the killings stopped.

The next Sunday, we were right there in the back of the church and Chuck was right beside of us. Lee decided to take over the sermons for awhile and pick up the pieces of the church. I didn't know if this was just a ploy to get us where they could watch us or if it was just so we could see where they were coming from.

Lee started out by welcoming us just like any other church would. The whole service though was kind of like any other church service would have been. It seemed normal, even down to the worship music and praising during the music.

   I did notice though when he started preaching he kept looking at us. It wasn't any normal sermon either, he was preaching about Adam and Eve but he kept talking more about the snake in the garden. It wasn't normal information either, he kept saying things like "that snake wasn't alone he had his mate and they corrupted the word of God. They were all over the garden, in the grass, in the rocks, in the sand, the ground, and in the trees. They were all around the garden and causing a commotion among the animals that Adam and Eve were to watch over."

   This was what seemed to be pointed at Julia and me alone. I couldn't prove it of course but, it seemed awfully coincidental that he kept looking at us and we had been upsetting the routine of the church. We were singled out, to say the least.

   I didn't care if he talked about us like that or not but, if anyone picked up on it they may try something and it would be him and Lynn keeping their word not to bother us. Although it would be someone in the church, even if it wasn't them directly.

The next Sunday wasn't any different, only a different part of the bible. It was about Moses and how he was persecuted by the pharaoh and his wife. It just continued from the Adam and Eve sermon. Every Sunday, it would be the same thing every time. A woman and a man causing havoc with a biblical hero, prophet, or martyr. This went on for at least two or three months and I don't think anyone caught on to what he was saying, at least right then.

It was about a month and a half after he stopped the finger pointing sermons that we found a note on our cars telling us to stop coming to the church if we knew what was good for us. Of course we couldn't quit if we wanted to be left alone, even though we weren't being let alone now. I confronted Lee in his office one weekday about the note and the sermons and he said to ignore it and that he had nothing to do with the note. I didn't believe him of course but, I had to act like I did and keep calm.

The day we found the notes I asked Julia to move in with me for protection. After all I have a big house and a couple of bedrooms that she could stay in. She, of course, chose the one closest to me so I would be near enough to protect her.

The first night though, she came into my room and asked if she could sleep with me. My answer was definitely yes, why wouldn't it be though. I mean, we had already had sex and slept in the same bed almost every night for the last couple of months.

We were staying together every night not just for protection but, I think we were falling in love. This I found out later to be a big mistake, sort of.

The next sermon was a little better because he let up on the persecution of us and focused on getting along with others.

Of course, this didn't last very long at all. A few sermons later he started back with the couple causing problems again. I don't know if he had forgotten our conversation or if he just was leading us on before.

CHAPTER FOURTEEN: More death!!!

It wasn't long after the sermons started back that Julia and I noticed a man with a brand on his arm of a Greek symbol who had died of mysterious circumstances. There also wasn't a day that Julia and I weren't together. The hospital hired two new nurses and they were to be in the ER when we weren't, that way we could work the same shifts all the time. That was more convenient than not sleeping and having to work tired.

So when the person came in unconscious and died in the ER, we of course being on the late shift were the ones to see him. A few minutes after he passed away there were these two gentlemen dressed in black suits and ties, came in and asked about him. We asked if they were family and at that point they produced Federal Bureau of Investigation badges. Their names were John Rockford and Joseph Hickman.

I just advised them they would have to talk to the doctor on duty, which was Jim Mullins. I introduced them to him and they proceeded to a private room to discuss the deceased.

After what seemed to be hours, but was only minutes, the two agents came out of the room talking between themselves. Although they stopped as they walked near us and resumed once they were far enough past us for us not to hear.

Doctor Mullins, however, didn't come out of the room right away. Once he did though he was scratching his head and had a bewildered look on his face.

I asked him what that was all about and all I got was "beats me!"

He started telling us about how the conversation went and how weird it was for them to inquire about the brand on the deceased. When I mentioned about the others, he just told me "Stop right there, I don't want to know any more! Maybe you should go talk to the agents since you know so much about the stuff!"

I took his advice and ran out of the ER and flagged down the agents and asked them about the brand on the deceased. They told me there was a nationwide investigation into a cult that brands people for trying to expose them for what they are, a cult. I asked what was the cult and they said it was the YOU movement and to stay clear of them at all costs. Of course they hadn't had the experience and hadn't found out what I had.

   The agents asked if I had any information about them, I told them I had a folder about an inch and half thick on them and had managed to go to the church without becoming a member all because they found out I knew about them.

   When I said this the one agent in shock told me I was coming with them and grabbed me by the arm. I pulled away and said "If I am, then so is Julia!" He asked me why and I told him, all because we had both done this together. The other agent walked back into the hospital and a few minutes later came back out with Julia beside him. We all got into the black Tahoe they were driving and rode to the hotel in Norton, where they were staying.

   The moment we arrived at their room we noticed a few other agents that were there as well. This seemed to be a very big operation going on.

They didn't waste any time asking all the wrong questions for me to answer. Things like what was our involvement and how did we fit into the picture. The most we could tell them was that they were on the right track and that there were several in on the murders. They knew we weren't telling them everything because they had someone who had dealt with them. The next thing I knew, Jack came walking in and said, "Guys, tell them all you have found. They already know what you have done so far and what all I have done.

Someone had forgotten to mention that Jack was not only ex-special forces but, was also FBI. This came to me as a shock, after all, he did hold someone captive and interrogate them.

After explaining all Julia and I had found out and what had happened before Jack had gotten involved, they seemed shocked. Jack didn't know about everything and it seemed as if the other agents were surprised as to us still being alive.

One agent handed me a file marked top secret and told me there was no turning back once I opened it. As I opened the file I saw the two bikers in it and both had been Navy Seals. I understood right then and there, I had been really lucky. These guys were no joke and I beat the odds because they thought I was just some dumb hillbilly with a gun. It does explain, however, how they were able to disarm the traps so easily at the big cabin. The file also had in it about their dishonorable discharge for doing "odd and strange things to prisoners of war" while transporting and holding them.

The file also explained about their blatant disrespect for the life of others and disregard for their fellow soldiers. These two just like I had learned were no Boy Scouts and definitely not someone to take lightly. Of course, we didn't and we overcame them.

There were more files that were handed to me and Julia that were marked classified and had more information about several of the main members of YOU.

This being said, we still knew more than the FBI about the group.

While we were there two of the agents advised that there were more strange deaths that had occurred within the last 24 hours. There were at least three they knew of within a hundred mile radius, two of which were just found and the other happened less than an hour ago. One had the symbol for Hades, another the symbol for Zeus, and the other had both the symbol for YOU and the symbol for Mercury.

The one who had the symbol for Hades, they died of smoke inhalation from their house catching fire and it was extinguished before it got to them. The one with Zeus was electrocuted trying to rewire an electrical outlet. Then there was Mercury, this one was kind of odd because they had just bought a nice new Corvette and wrapped it around a tree doing 120 and lost control when they couldn't slow down for a curve.

All of these seemed to be one hundred percent valid...

...except for the brands on them.

CHAPTER FIFTEEN: The Takedown!!!

All of the evidence the FBI had pointed to Lynn and Lee without a doubt. They had just one problem, to catch the two of them in the act themselves.

The FBI needed bait, they needed someone on the inside, they needed unfortunately...

...us!

I just knew this wouldn't turn out to the good. When they asked, well, when they told us we were going to do this for them, Julia at first said no. Then when they told us the group would never know who turned them in but, we were just under investigation and were being followed. The best cover story I had heard so far.

   The whole idea was for us to go to Lee and Lynn and tell them that we had decided not to keep quiet about the whole incident there. When they tried to take us somewhere to get rid of us the FBI would follow us and arrest them. There would be a tracker embedded in our skin so small it couldn't be detected. That way if they lost us, the agents would be able to go right to where we were.

   While this wasn't the best-laid plans it seemed the best I had heard out of anyone to take the two lunatics down. We prepared everything and the trackers were placed in our butt cheeks as to look as if we had received shots for inoculation of diseases. We also had fake airline tickets going out of the country with passports to back up the tickets. I told Jack that after this they'd better give us tickets to go out of the country for real and to a nice place.

   We gathered our things and got in a cab, which was driven by another agent, and headed back to the hospital to get my car. Once we arrived of course, we had to go explain ourselves and the agents assisted and gave a cover story of why we were taken away like we were.

When that was taken care of we loaded our things in the car and drove to my house and prepared for what was to come as much as we could.

We rested a few hours and decided it was time to go ahead and get it over with. After several times trying to psyche ourselves up for the next step, we decided to just go ahead and get it done. We got in the car and drove what seemed to be an hour or two but, was only fifteen minutes down the road to the church. Once there we both got out and approached the side door of the church, which we knew would be unlocked and walked in. We found our way to Lee's office and knocked on the thin wooden door. The echo sounded like I was beating it down, only I barely rapped on it.

A large, muscle-bound man answered the door and asked if he could help us. Lee told him to let us in and be nice about it. The brute moved aside and motioned us in. I didn't beat around the bush once we were in at all.

"Lee, I have to say this and you know what I am going to say don't you? We had an agreement for the killing to stop and it has started back up once again! You know what this means, don't you?" I asked him.

Lee however, as expected, took it very disrespectfully and started ranting about how we were ungrateful little pests who don't know how good they have it. His face was turning red as he spoke and his tone went from a low rumble to a higher pitched scream. At one point I thought he would pass out because his lips started turning blue then white from the lack of oxygen. The last words of his rant were to the gorilla like man "take them to the car and I will get Lynn!"

The oversized thug grabbed my arm and I jerked away and told him I could walk myself. We walked out to the vehicle parked out back of the building, got in, and waited on Lynn and Lee. As soon as Lynn got into the vehicle she smiled and said "I have been waiting on this since the day you guys took me to that little hole in the ground. This is going to be fun!"

We drove what seemed to be hours but it was only around an hour. The place we were going was an abandoned bread factory near Abingdon and Bristol. They had converted part of it into a church and the rest was just abandoned and run down.

The goon ordered us out of the vehicle. I got out and helped Julia out, which she was kind of reluctant to do so. Which was understandable, after all, we were the bait for a large operation trying to capture and prosecute Lee and

Lynn. Thing is about being bait, it doesn't always work out to the best for bait.

After we got out we were led into the factory, which smelled like a cross between death, mold, and yeasty bread. The smell would almost knock you down right along with the heat coming from inside. Once inside they led us to a little room off to the side which had a couple of metal chairs that looked as if they had been sitting in the weather for a couple of years. The two goons forced me to sit then began to tie Julia and myself to the chairs.

I remembered what Julia had said about getting tied up and forced my limbs away from the chair as much as I could to loosen the ropes while being bound. I really didn't want to take the chance of not having the trackers in our ass cheeks not working. Of course what happened next would kill that plan.

The one goon walked out of the room for just a few minutes and returned with a truck dolly that had a fairly large car battery and jumper cables. This was not going to be fun at all.

The other goon then reached over and unrolled a short hose and turned on a rusty faucet, then proceeded to soak us. Once we had been soaked thoroughly, Lynn walks in with rubber boots up to her knees and rubber gloves up to her elbows. With her dress she was wearing, she kind of resembled a Nazi SS torture agent, all she needed was the swastika and SS to be on her somewhere.

Lynn proceeded to attach the black negative lead to the leg of my chair and there was what looked like steel wool on the positive lead. She looks at me with an evil look, grins and says "I told you this was going to be fun, for me, not so much for you!"

When she touched the lead to my arm it felt as if someone had put a torch to that side of my body and set me on fire and my muscles just jerked and twitched uncontrollably until she removed the lead. I had welded before and used a wet glove but that was nothing compared to the feeling of the car battery, this was hell!!!

I started smelling shit and urine and realized it was mine. Lynn began to question us about who we had told. Of course my answer was "No one!" every time. She wasn't taking that as an answer so she in hooked the black lead and hooked it on Julia's chair. The look on her face I still remember, fear can been seen in anyone and her face showed sheer terror. I managed to mutter to her, "I am so, so sorry baby." and at that moment Lee walks in and asks for everyone to come with him. Of course Lynn, wanted to stay and have more "fun" but, he insisted that we weren't going anywhere.

As soon as they shut the door I started moving my arms and legs to try to get loose. Julia, however was loose in a matter of seconds and was helping me to get loose. Evidently the shocks had made my muscles think they were moving when they weren't budging. She helped me to my feet and we snuck out of another door.

The minute we did we heard the main door we had originally came in along with other doors burst open and someone say "FBI, stop where you are and put any weapon on the floor you're under arrest!"

I couldn't have been more relieved to hear someone else at that moment. There were agents who helped us to a vehicle and one of them even offered to lend me some clothing to change into after I cleaned up a bit. It was all over and Julia didn't get hurt. I was relieved most about that mainly.

CHAPTER SIXTEEN: The End Or So We Thought

After the trials of Lynn and Lee they were sentenced to several life sentences over at least 30 deaths linked to them and because of our testimonies. The only thing left was to move to another area and hopefully make a living at what ever we could. We were finally relocated to Tampa, FL where we worked from home as nurses consulting patients calling in after hours.

I wish though we had stayed in more often though.

One day we ventured out just to look around and go out to eat. This was a big mistake for we came across a church for YOU and one person outside that we saw had been at the trial...

...here we go again!!!

Made in the USA
Columbia, SC
21 August 2024

44319dd4-aba8-4484-8919-f128770654f9R01